Beautiful Faces

grayscale coloring book

curated by

Tabz Jones

FIRST EDITION 2016

TABZ JONES
PO BOX 2137
ALMA, AR. 72921
WWW.GOTHICTOGGS.NET

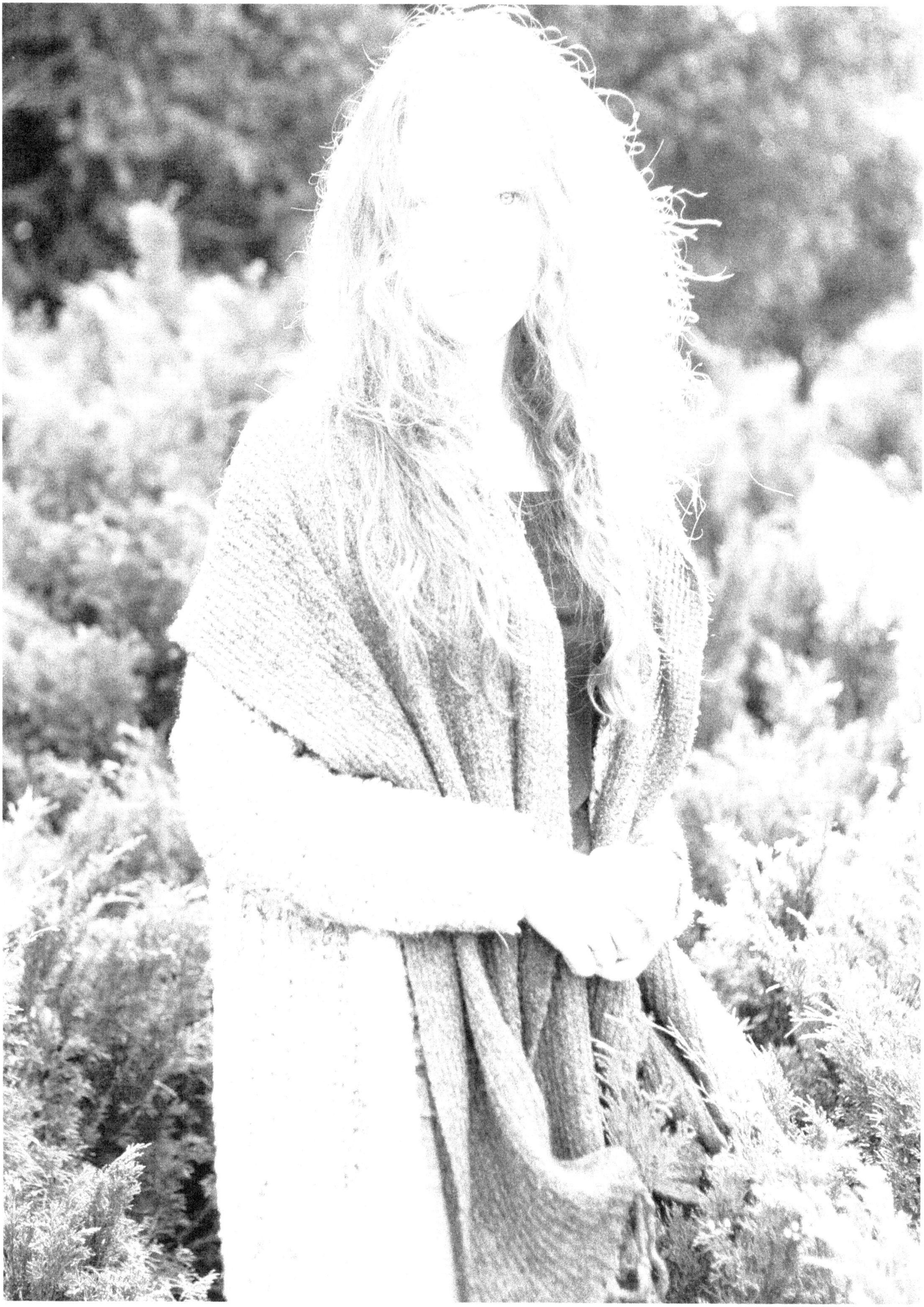

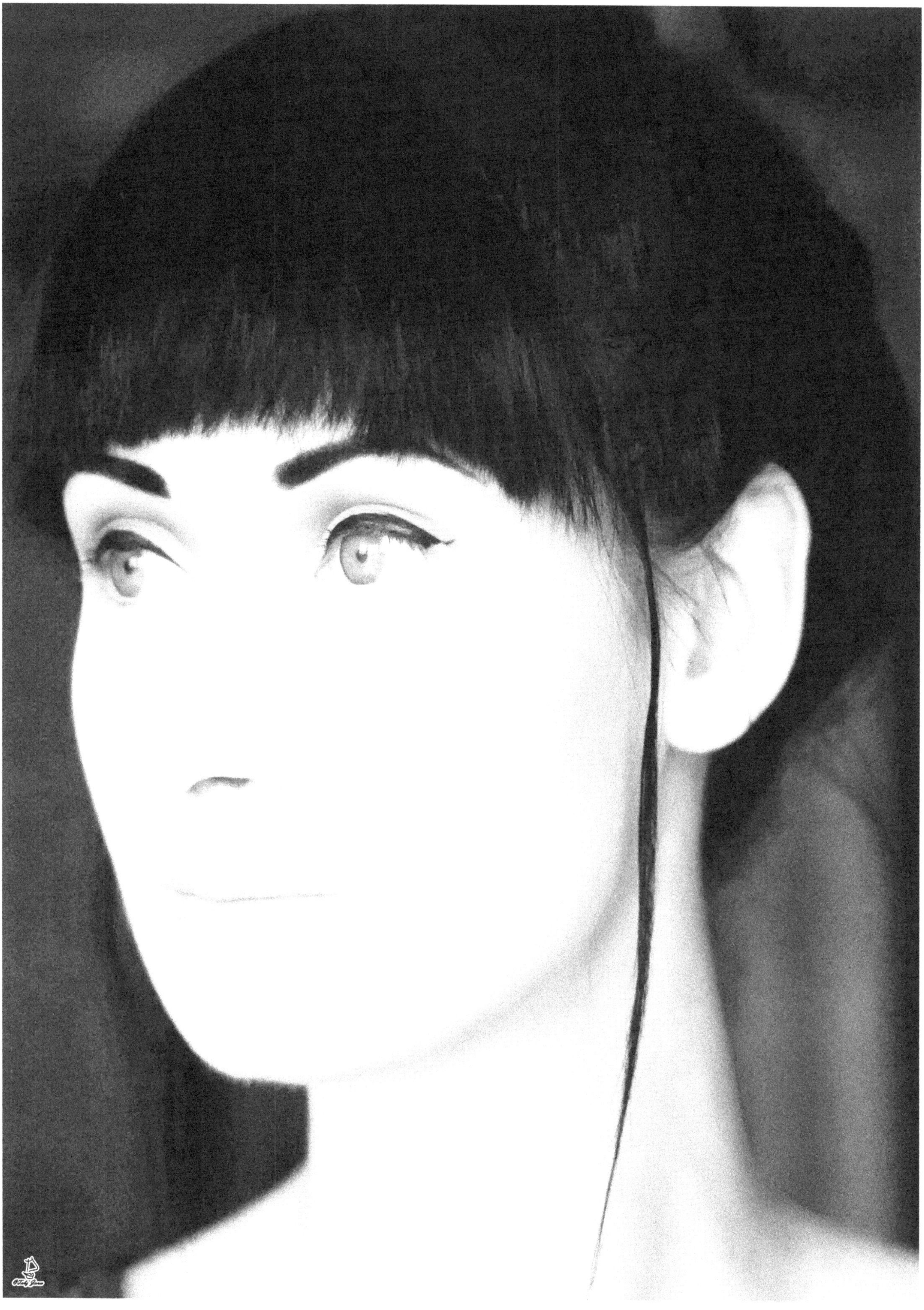

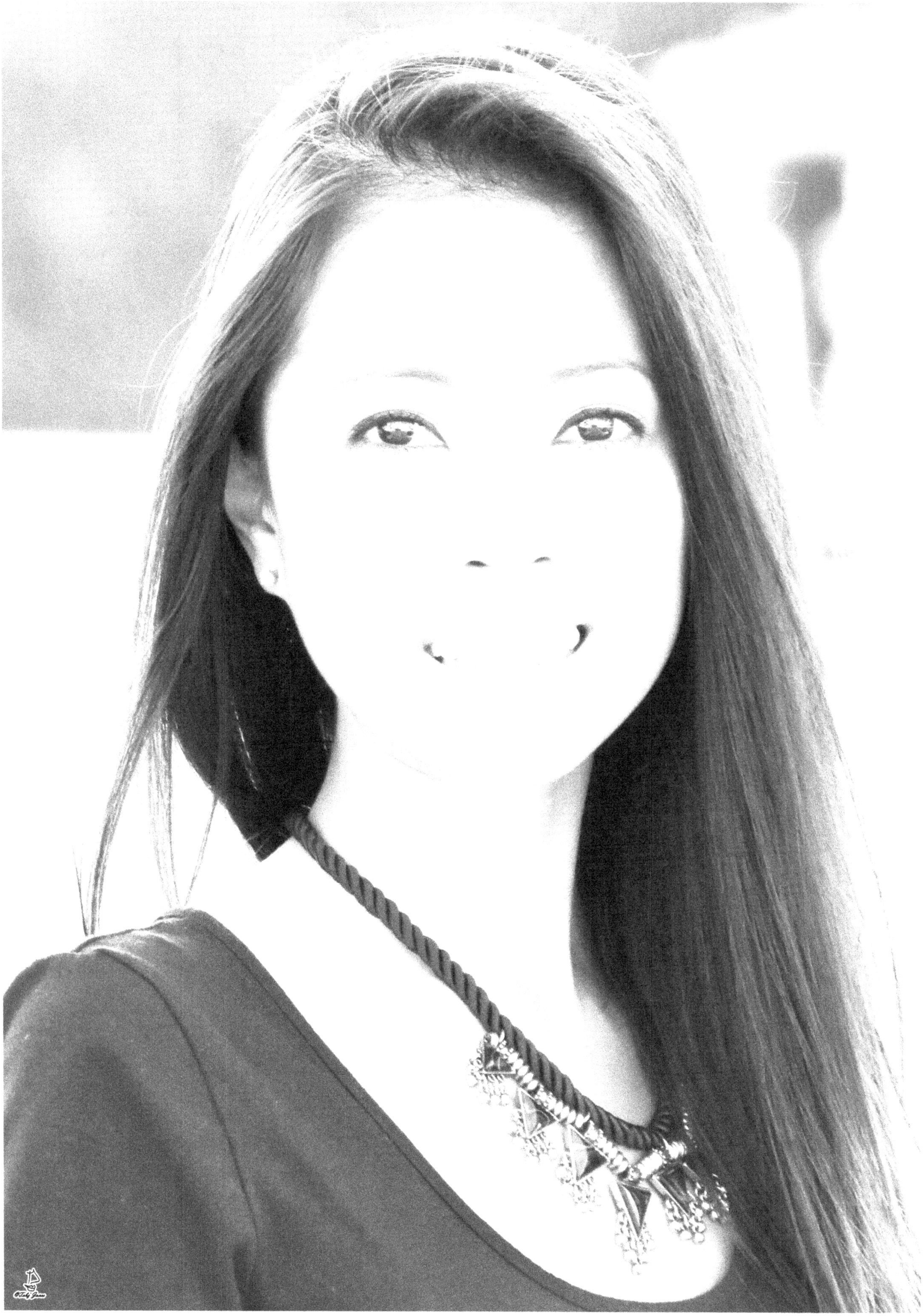

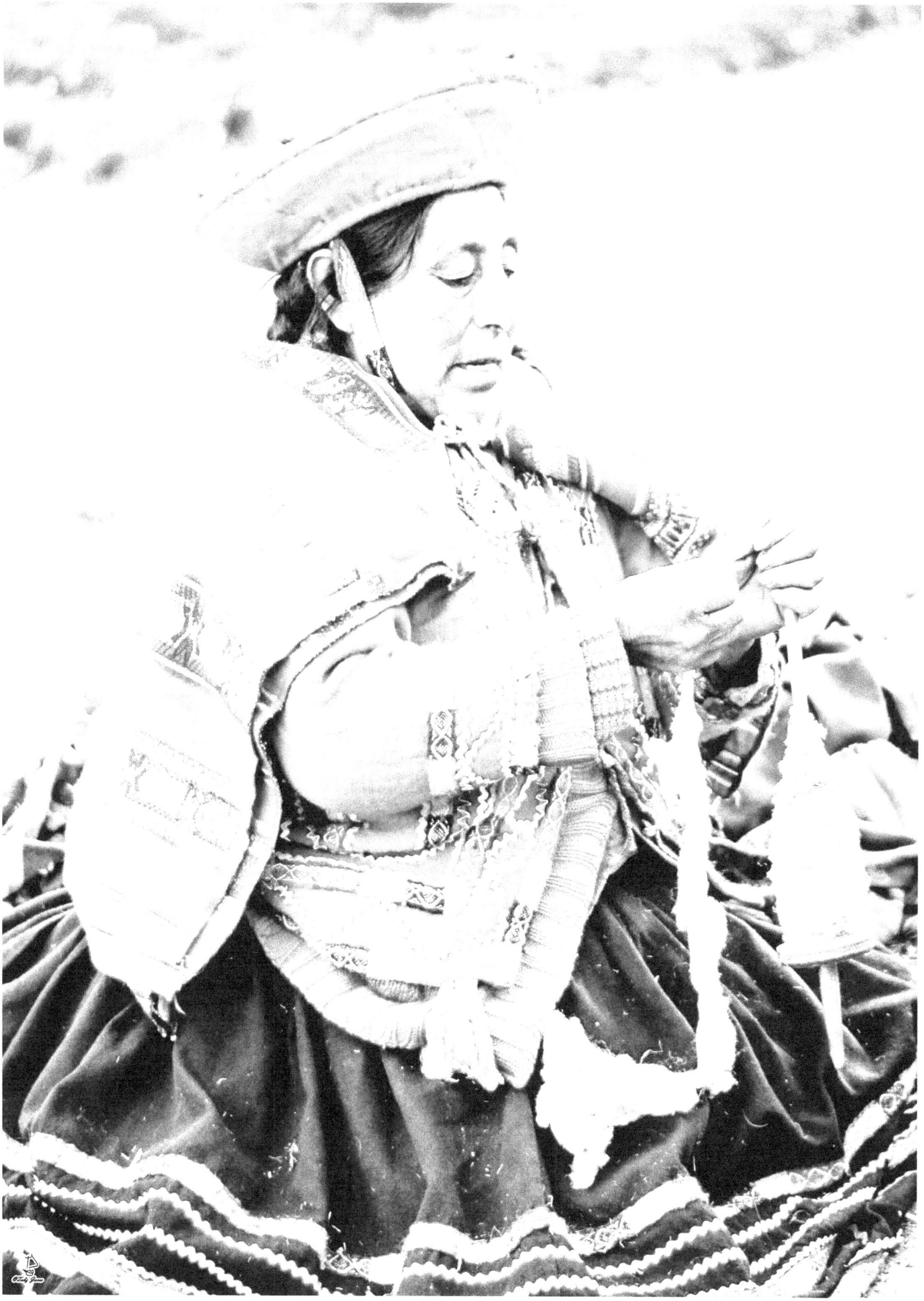

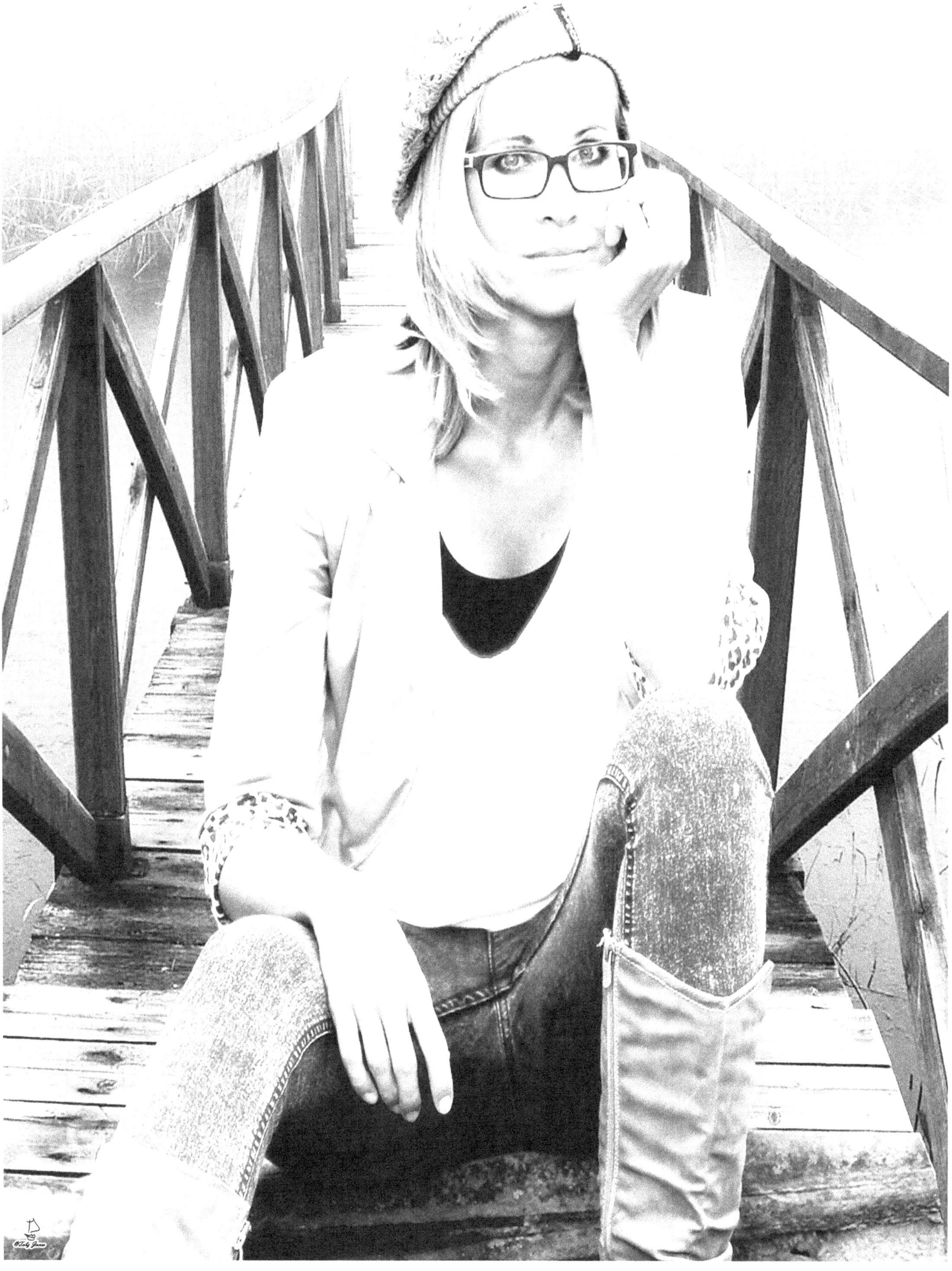

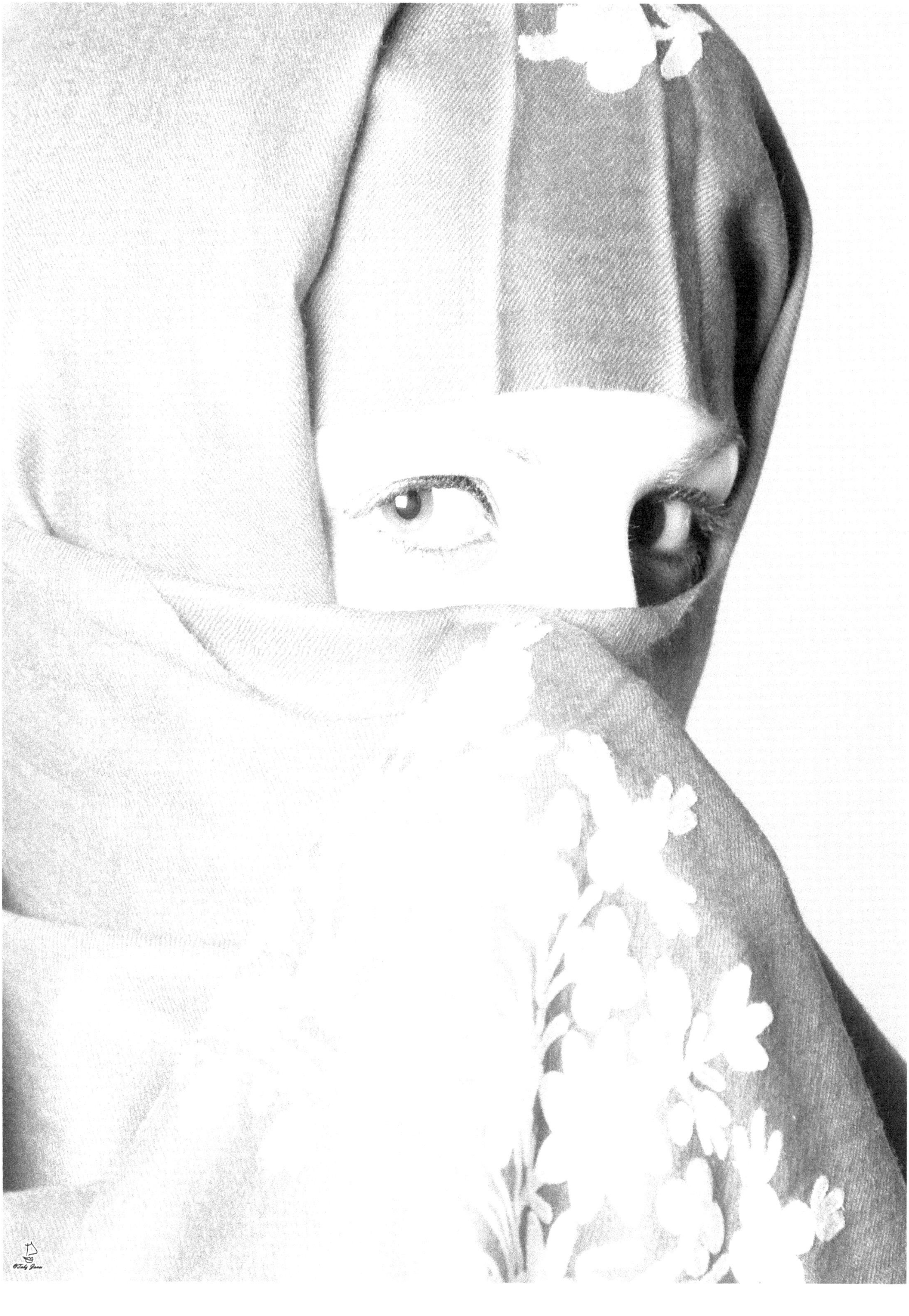

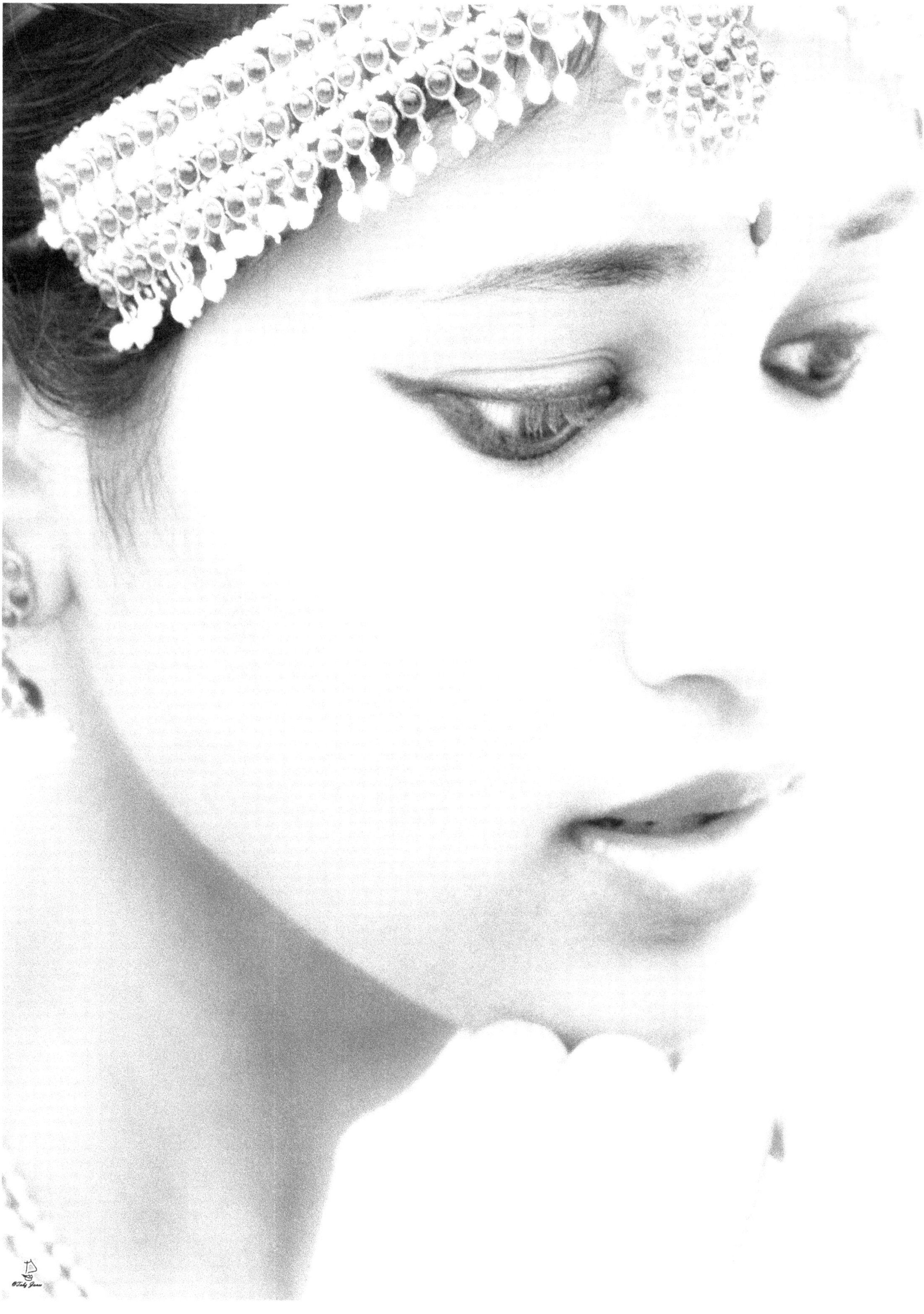

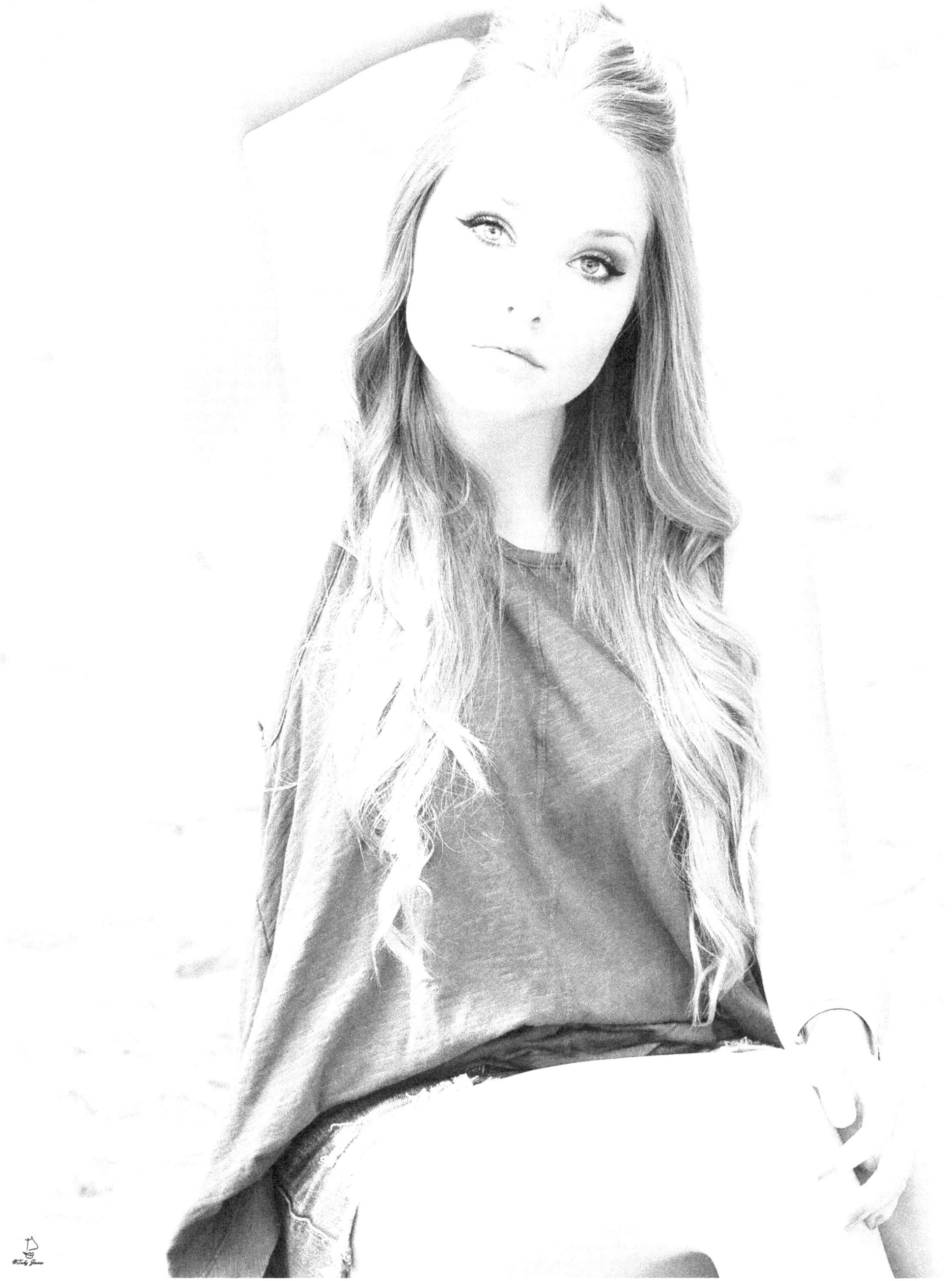

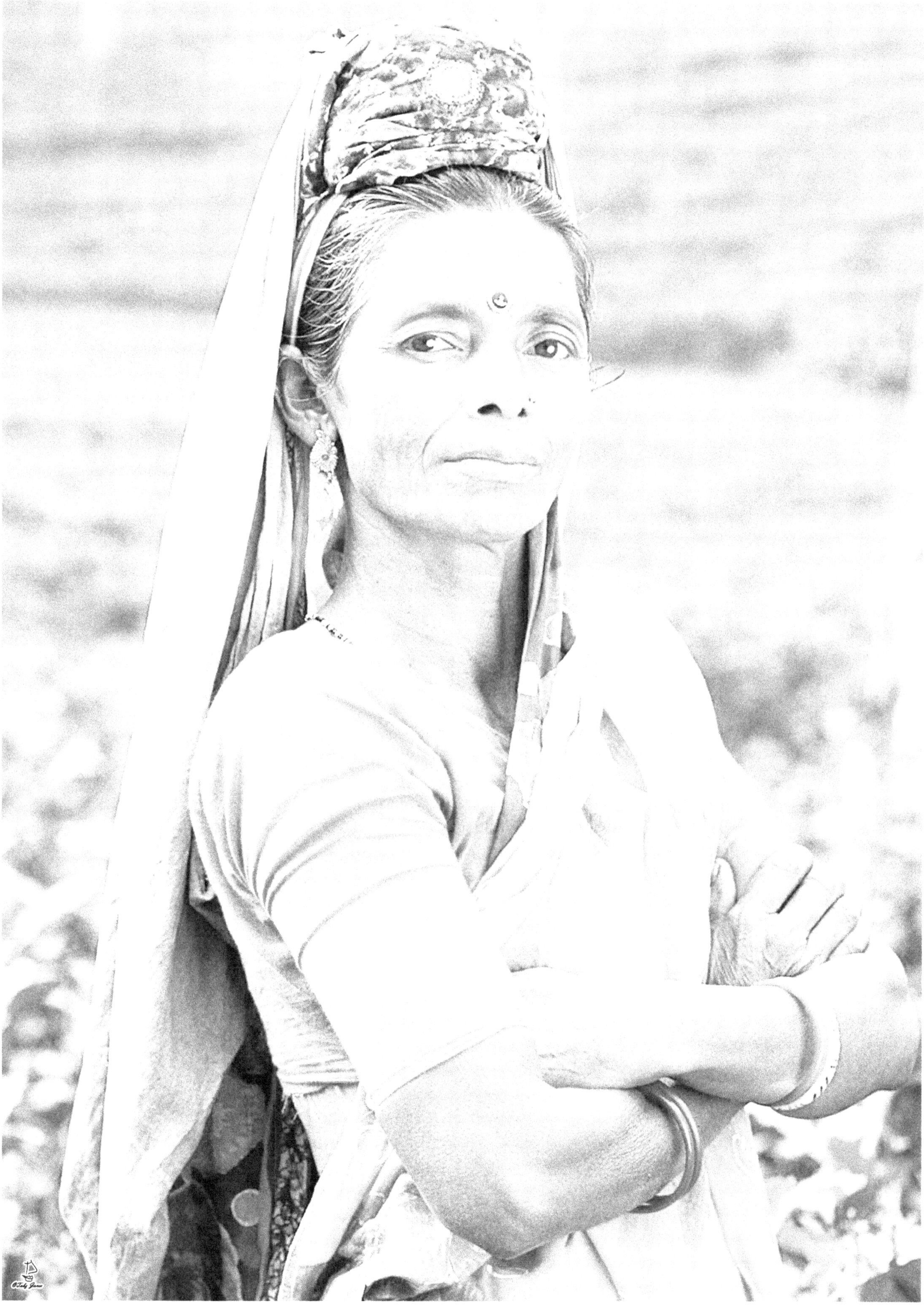

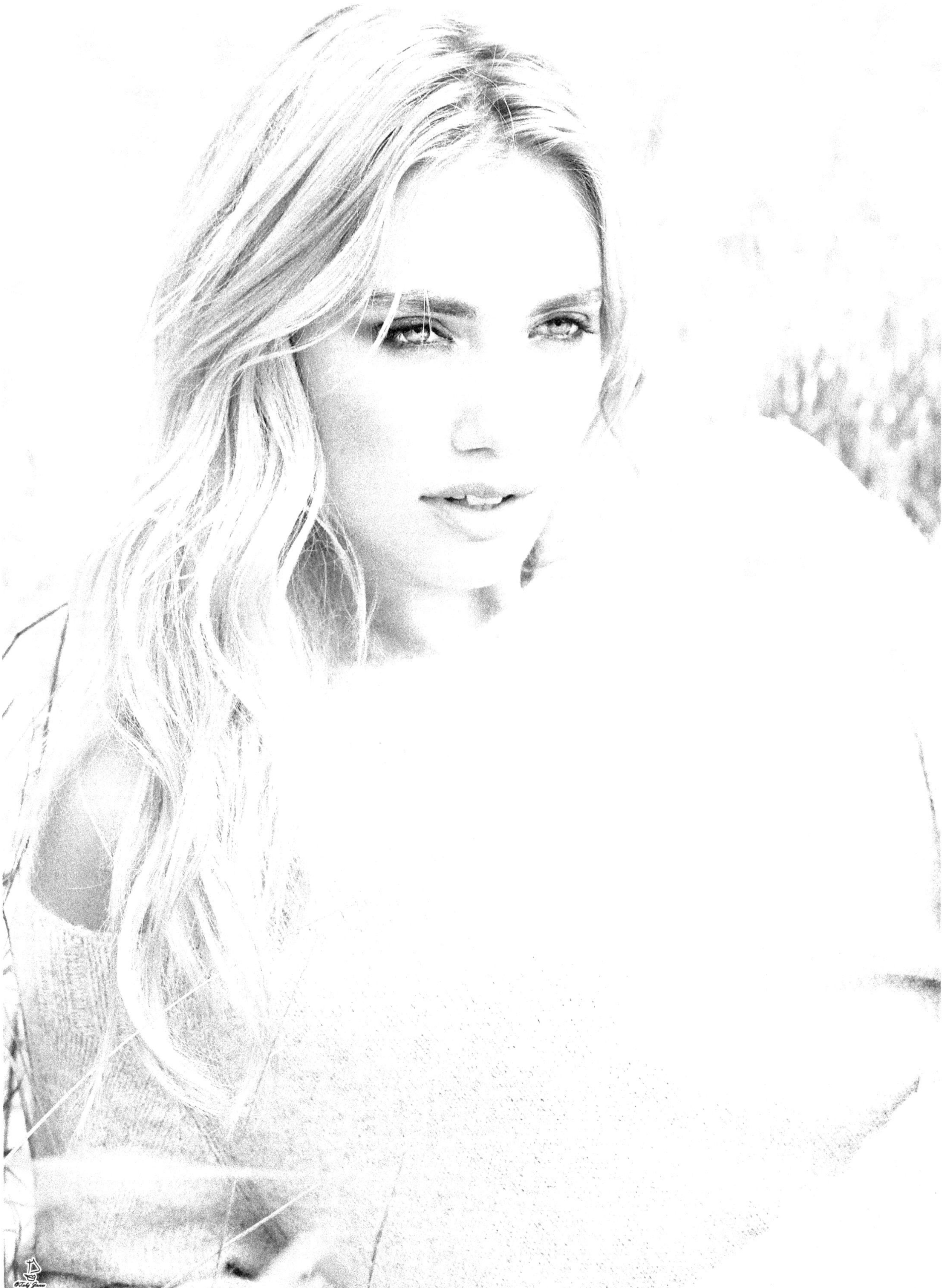

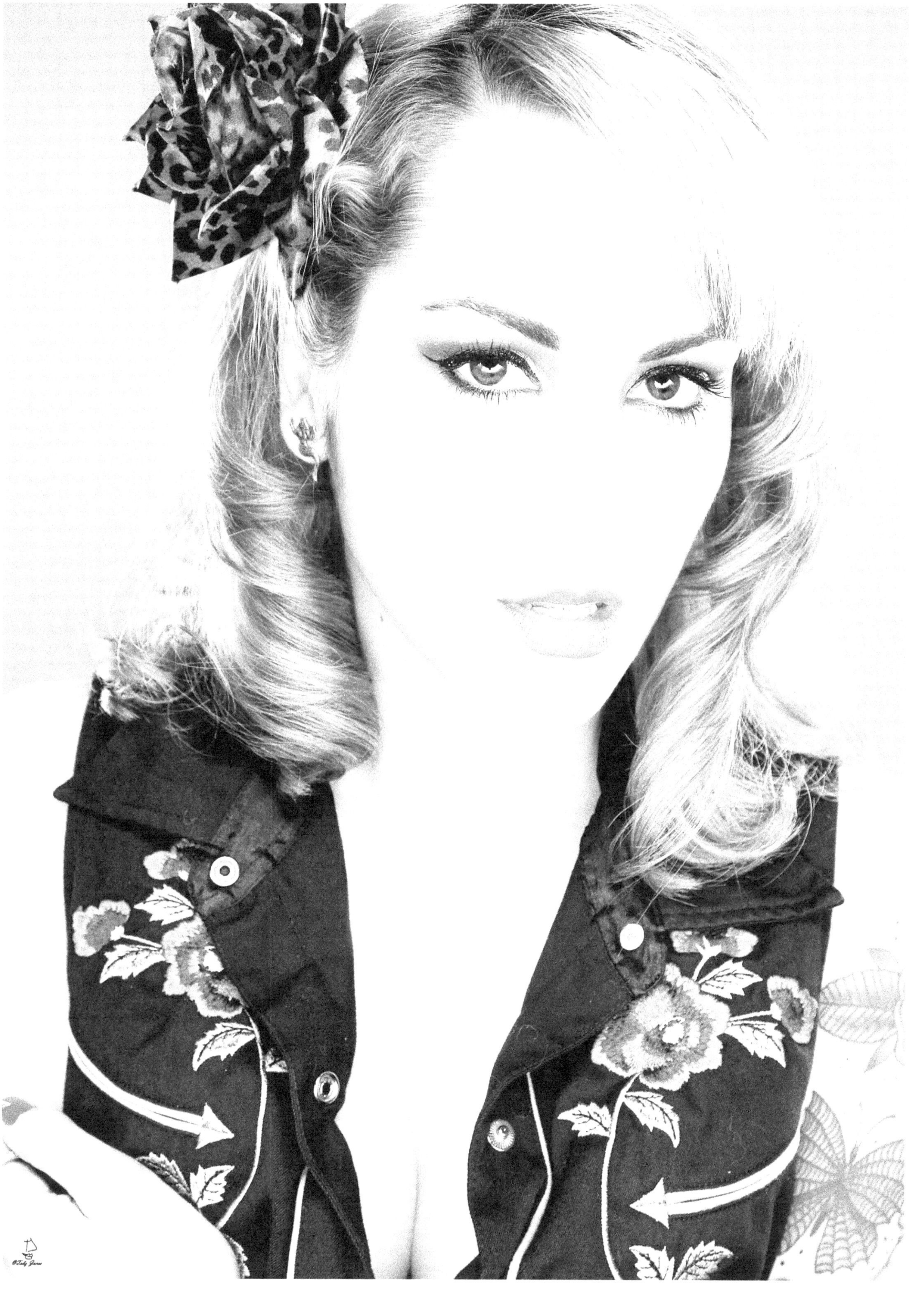

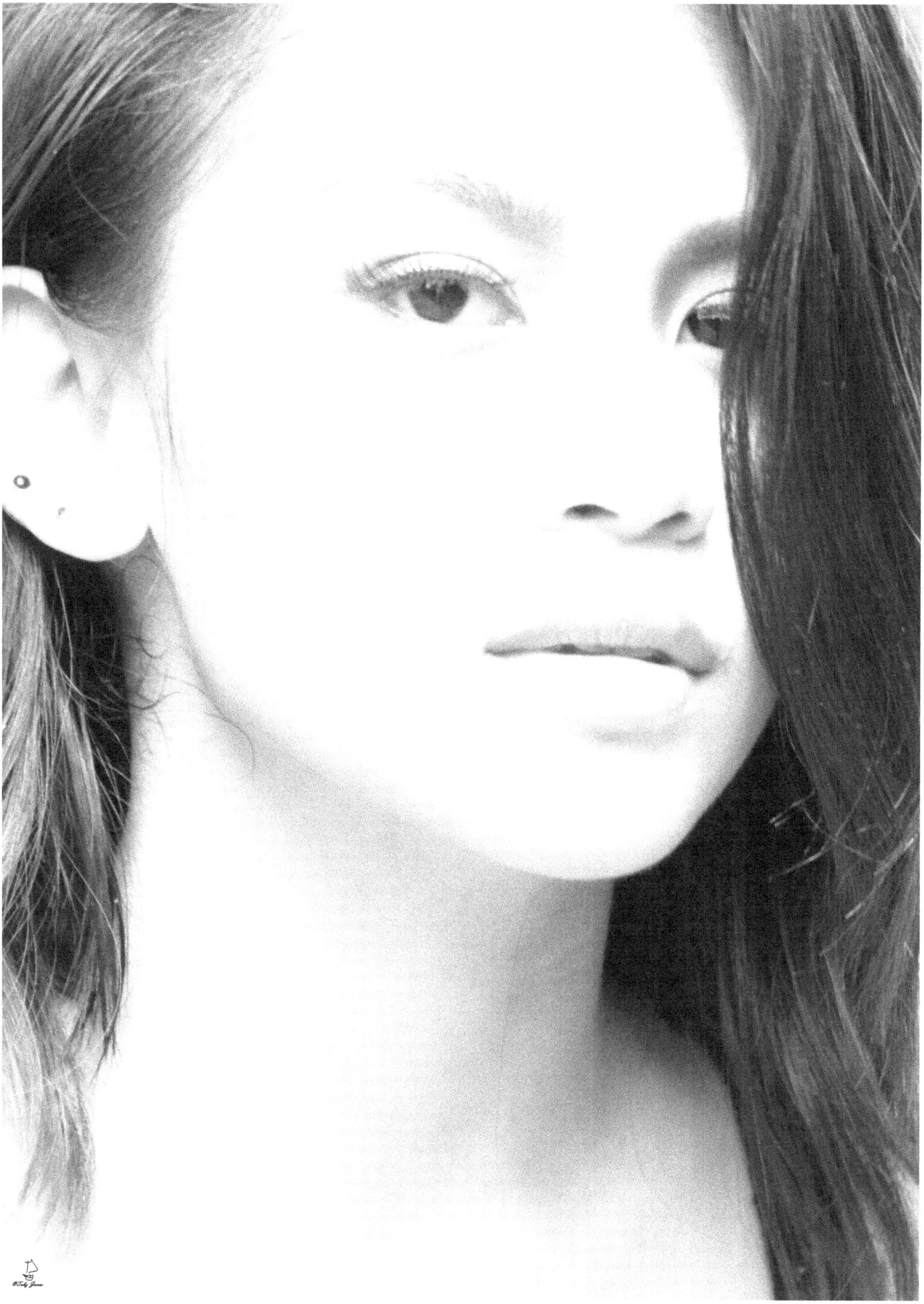

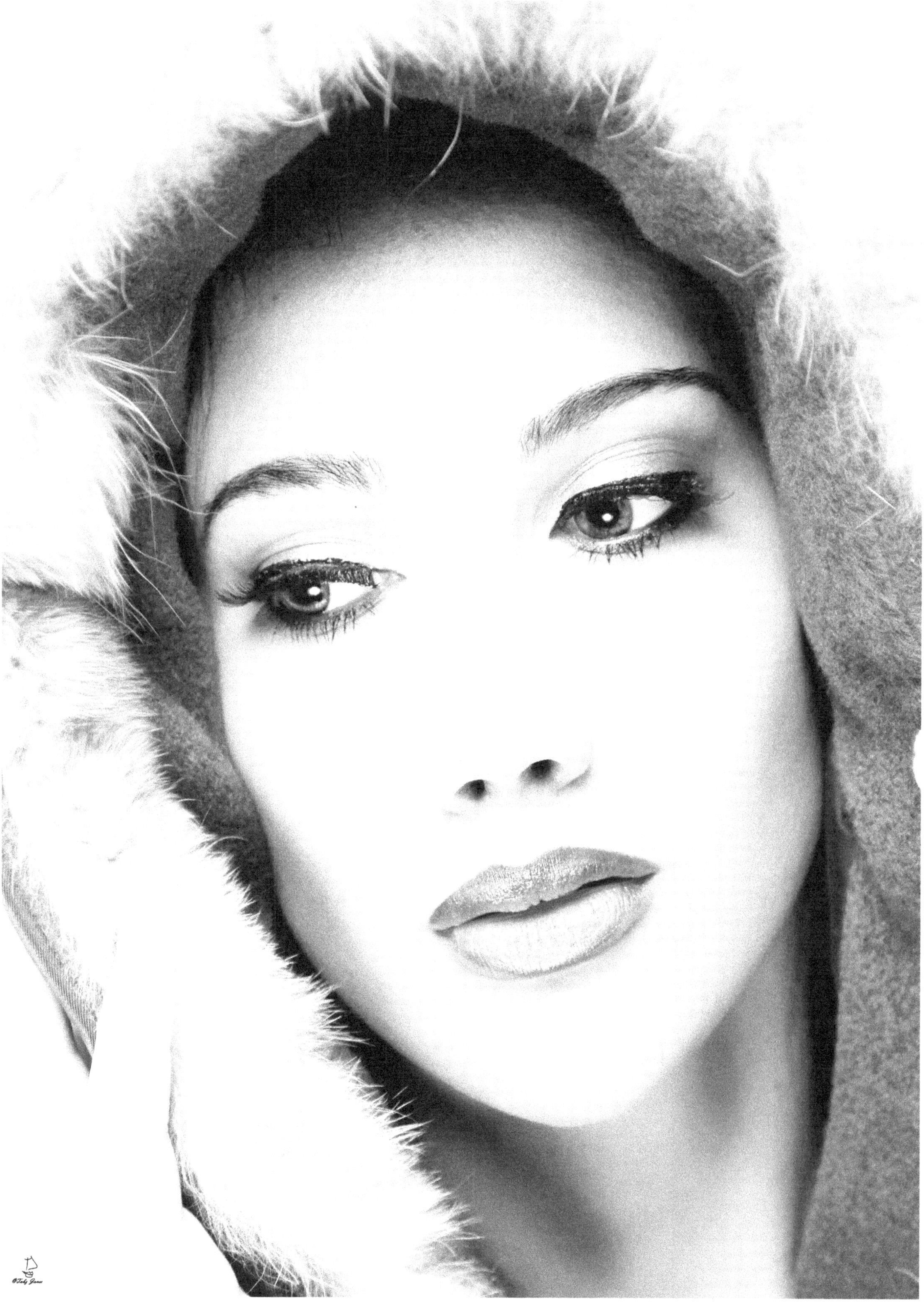

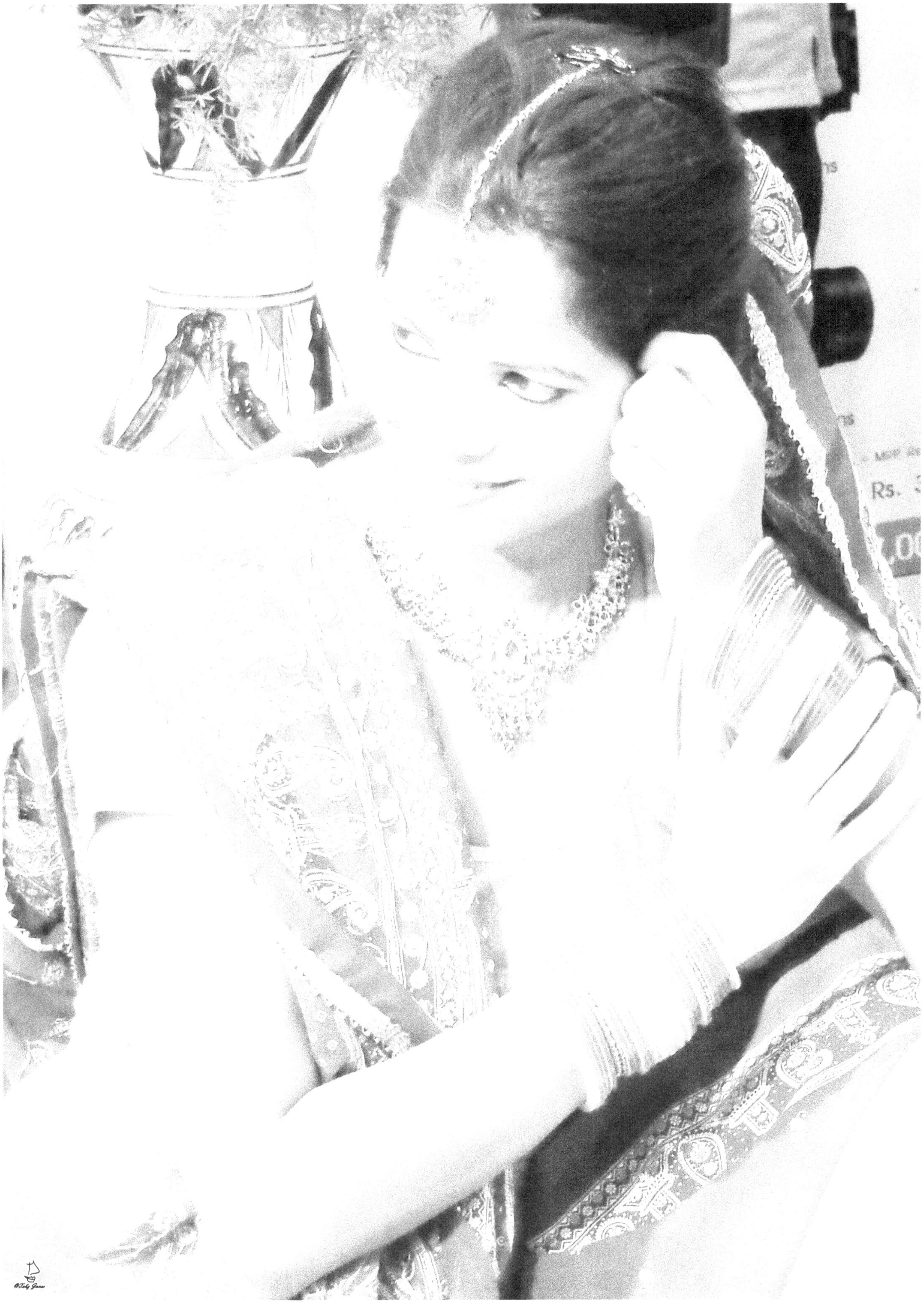
Rs.

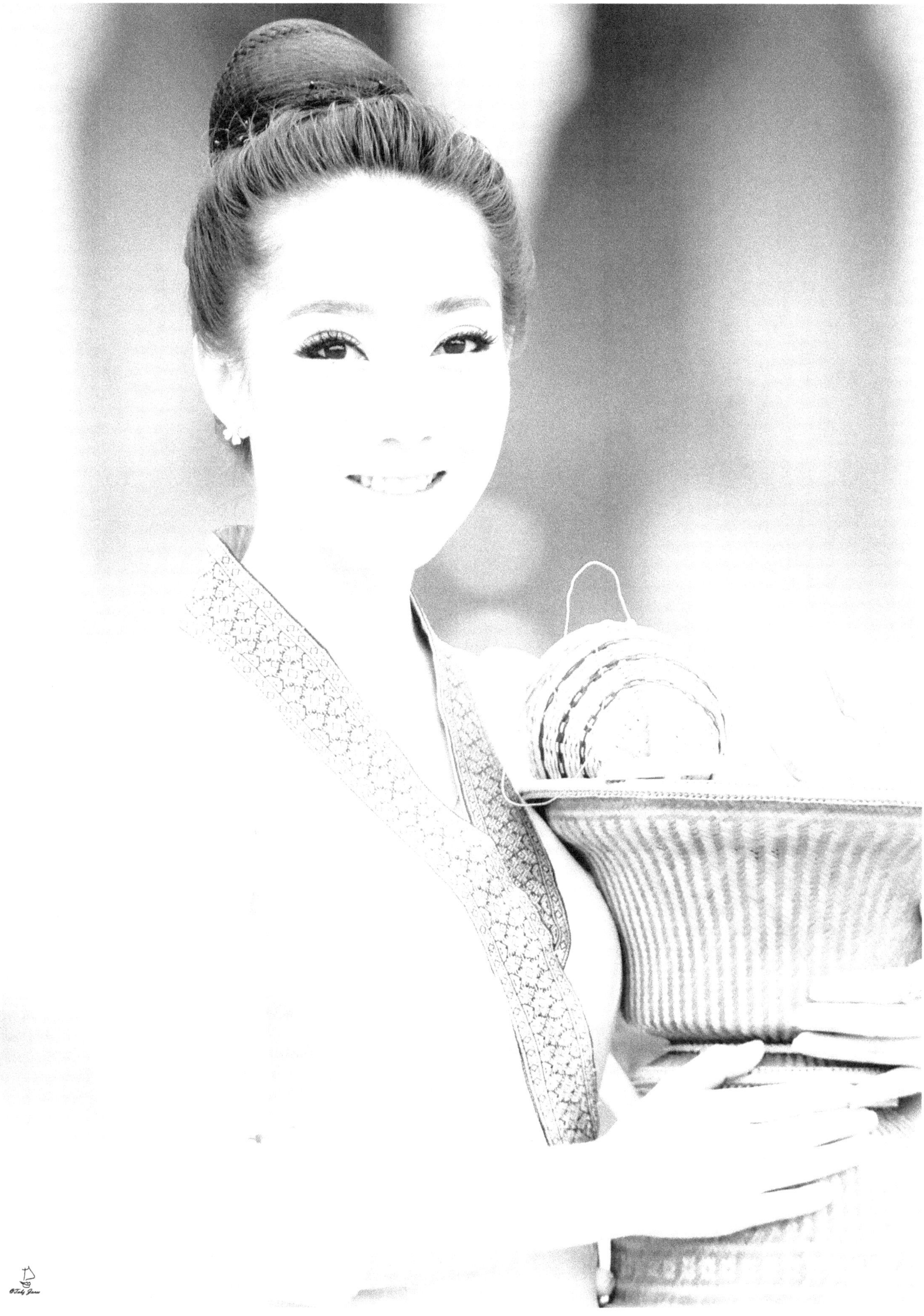

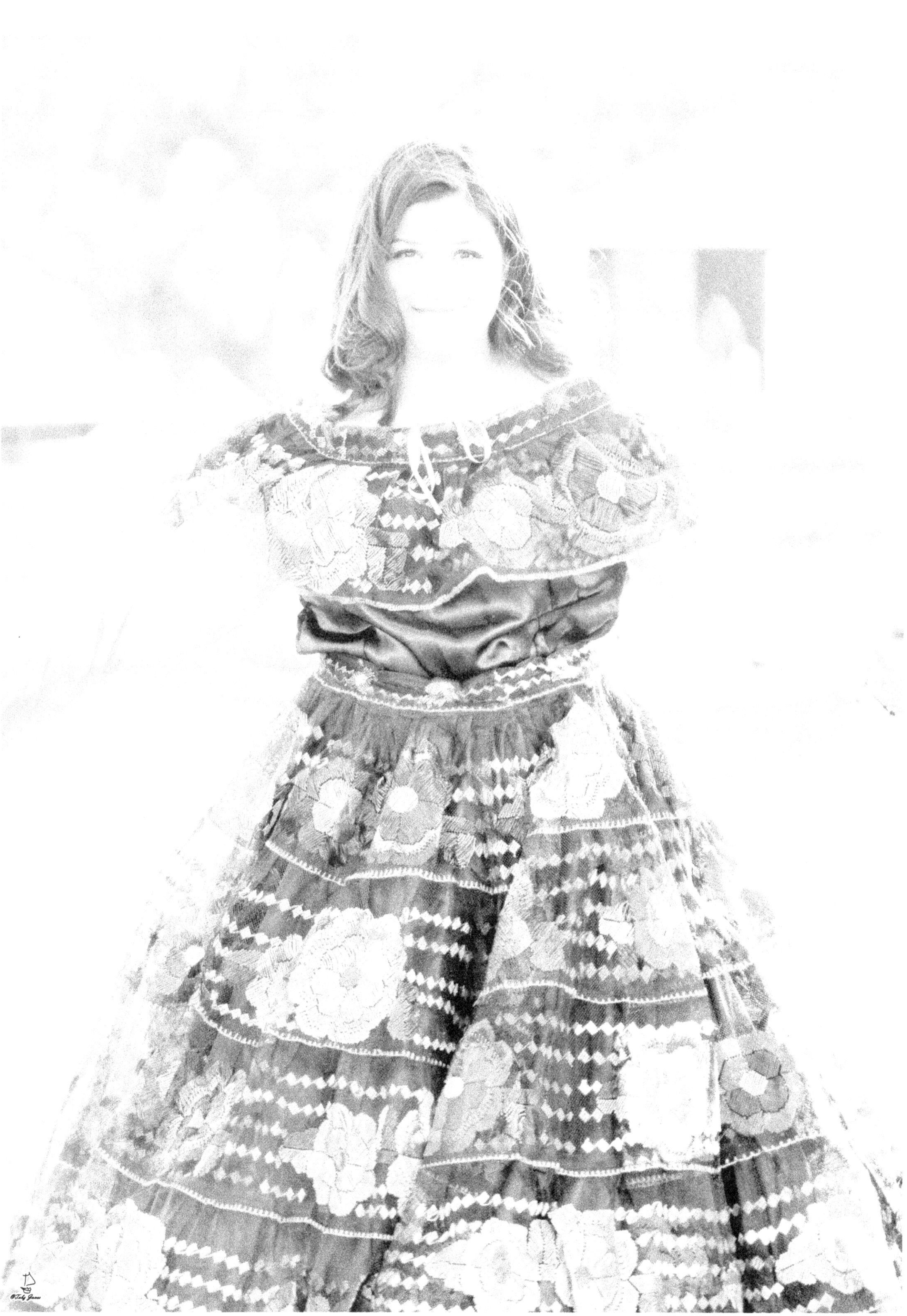

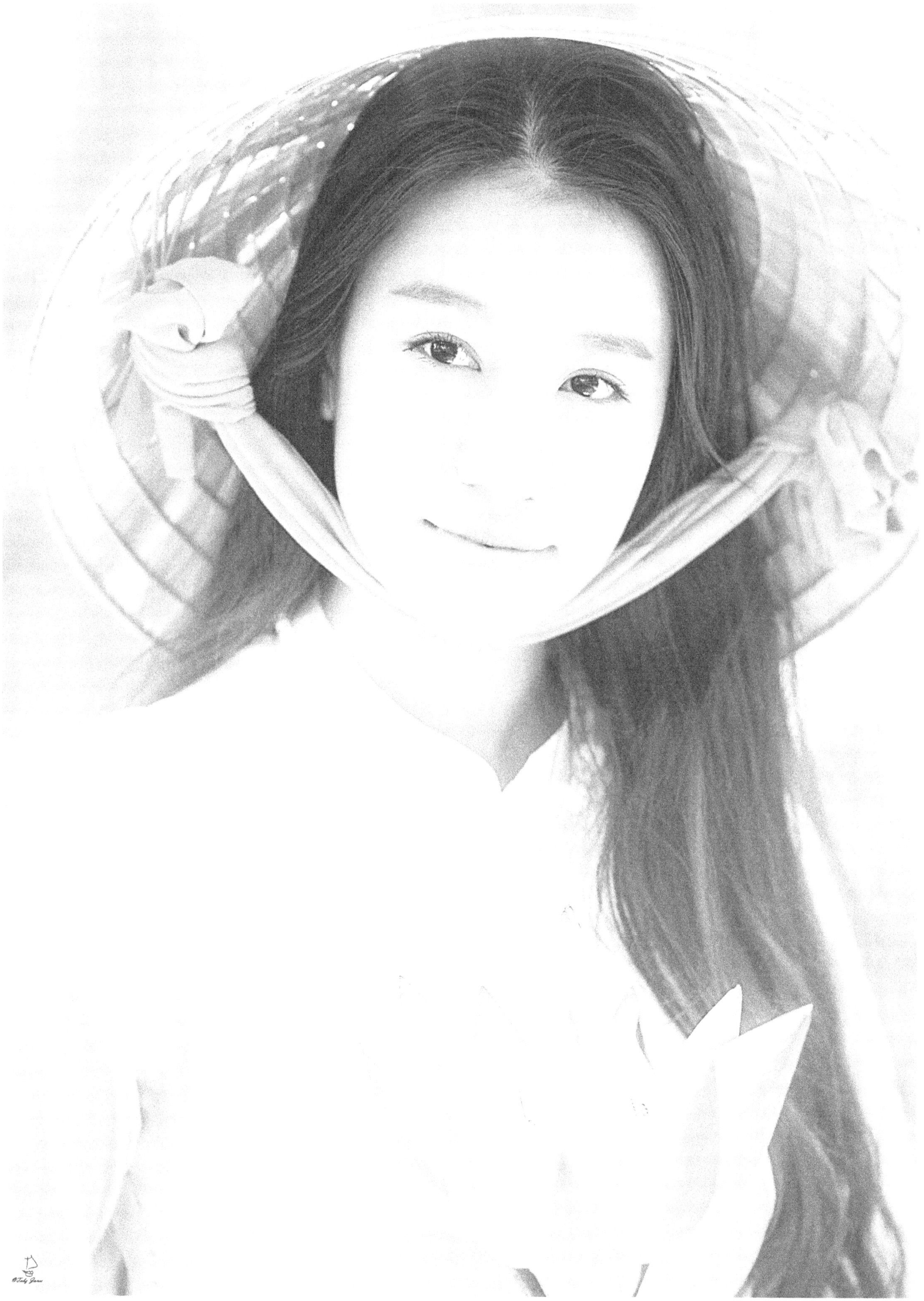

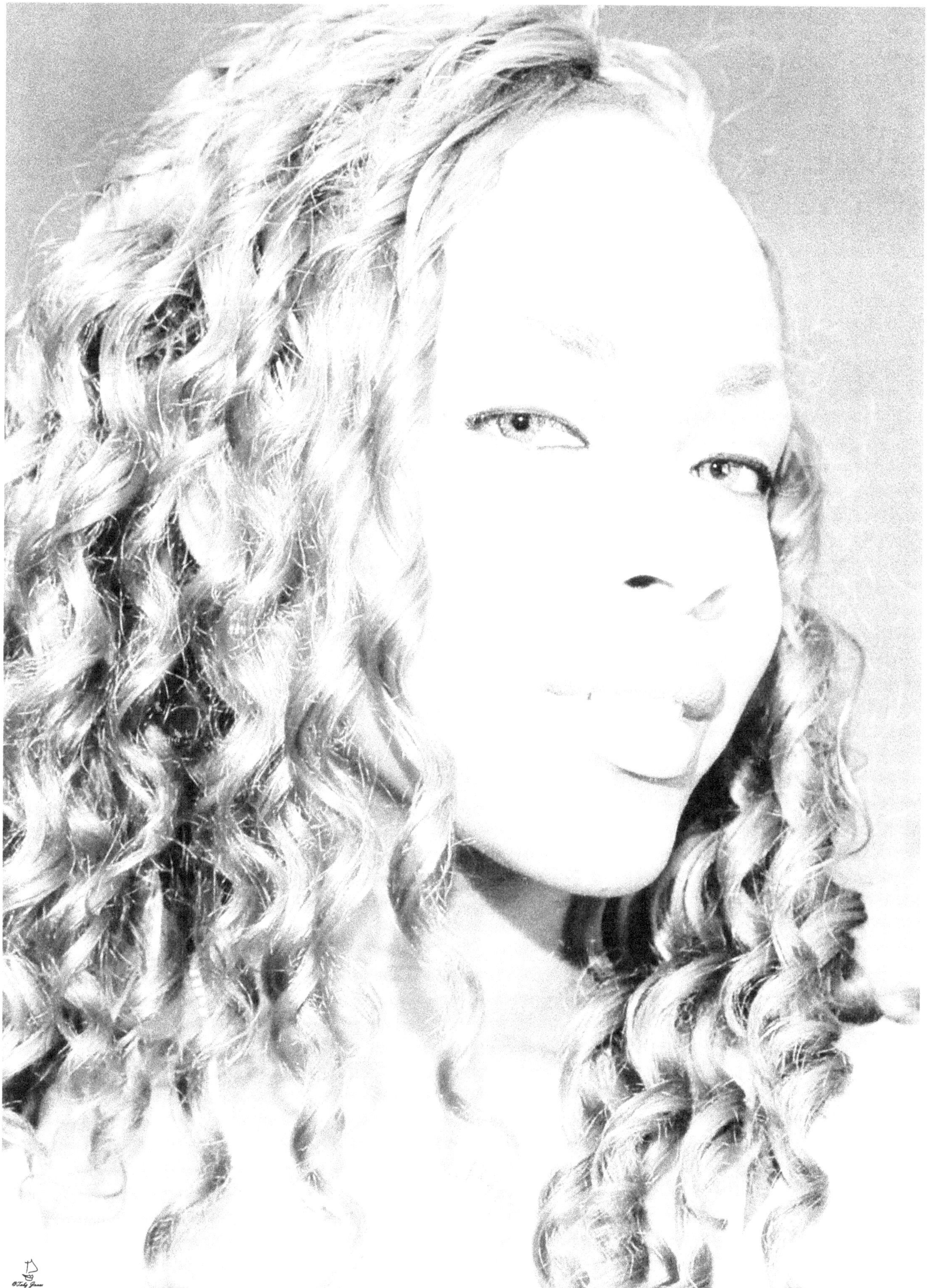

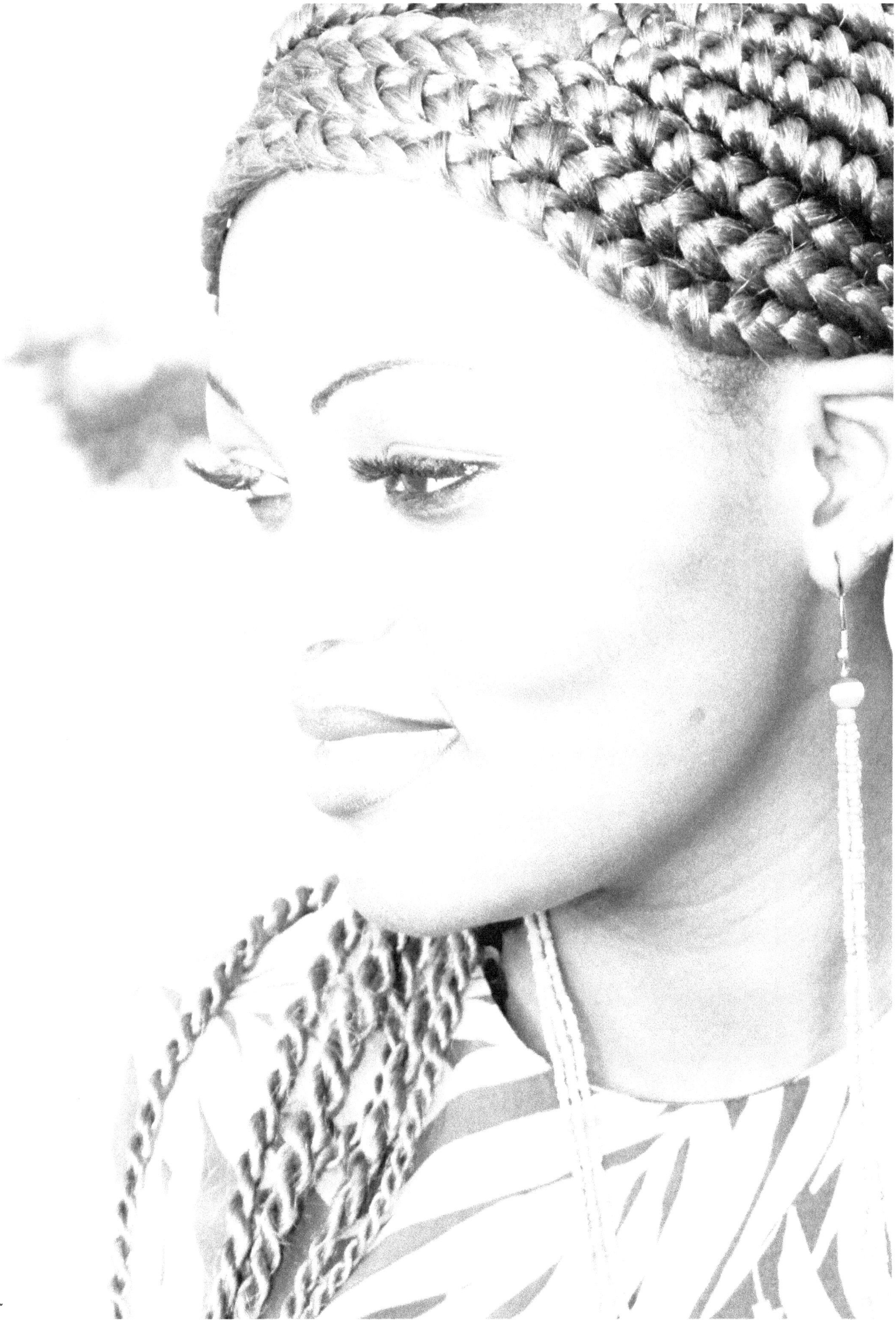

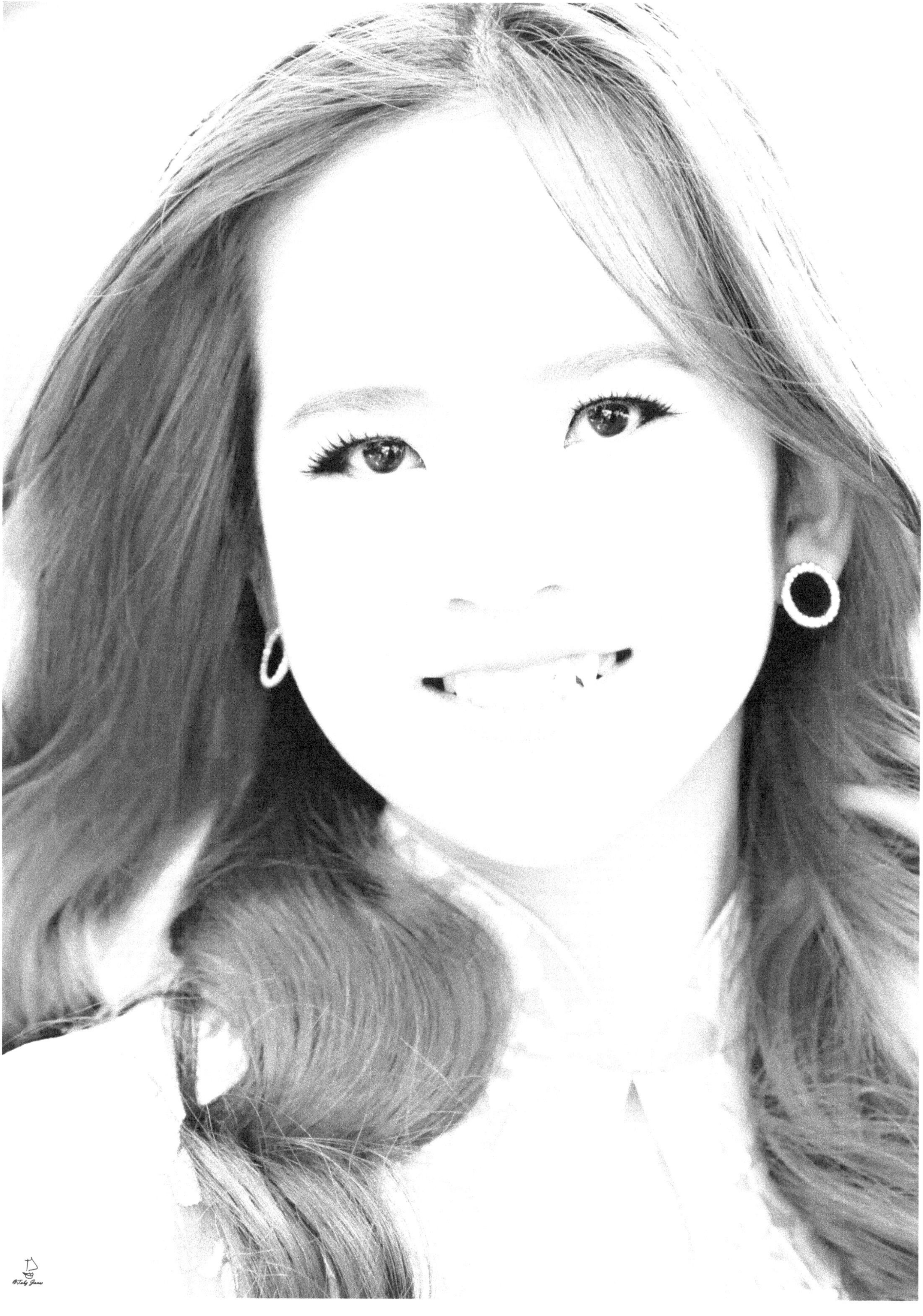

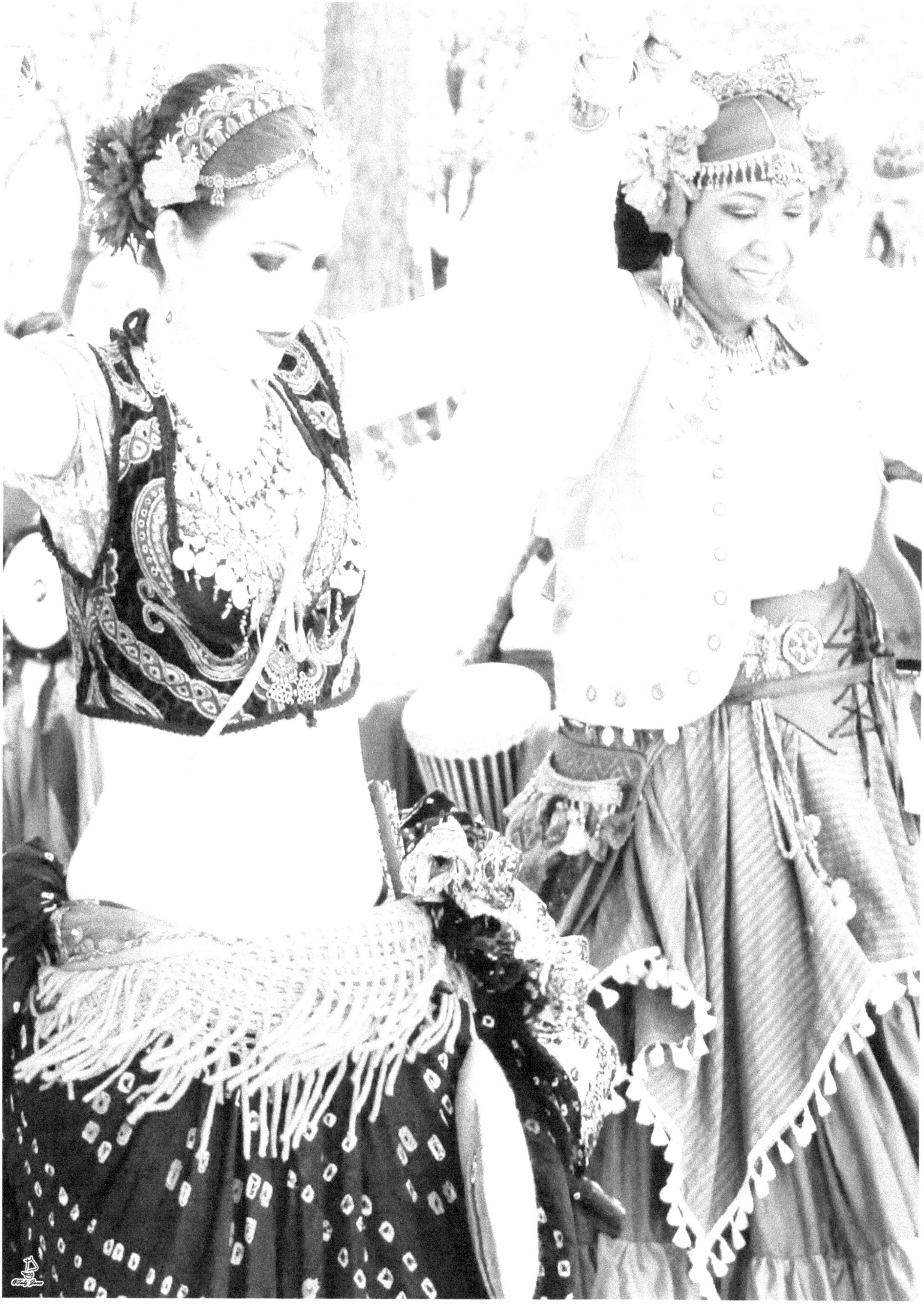

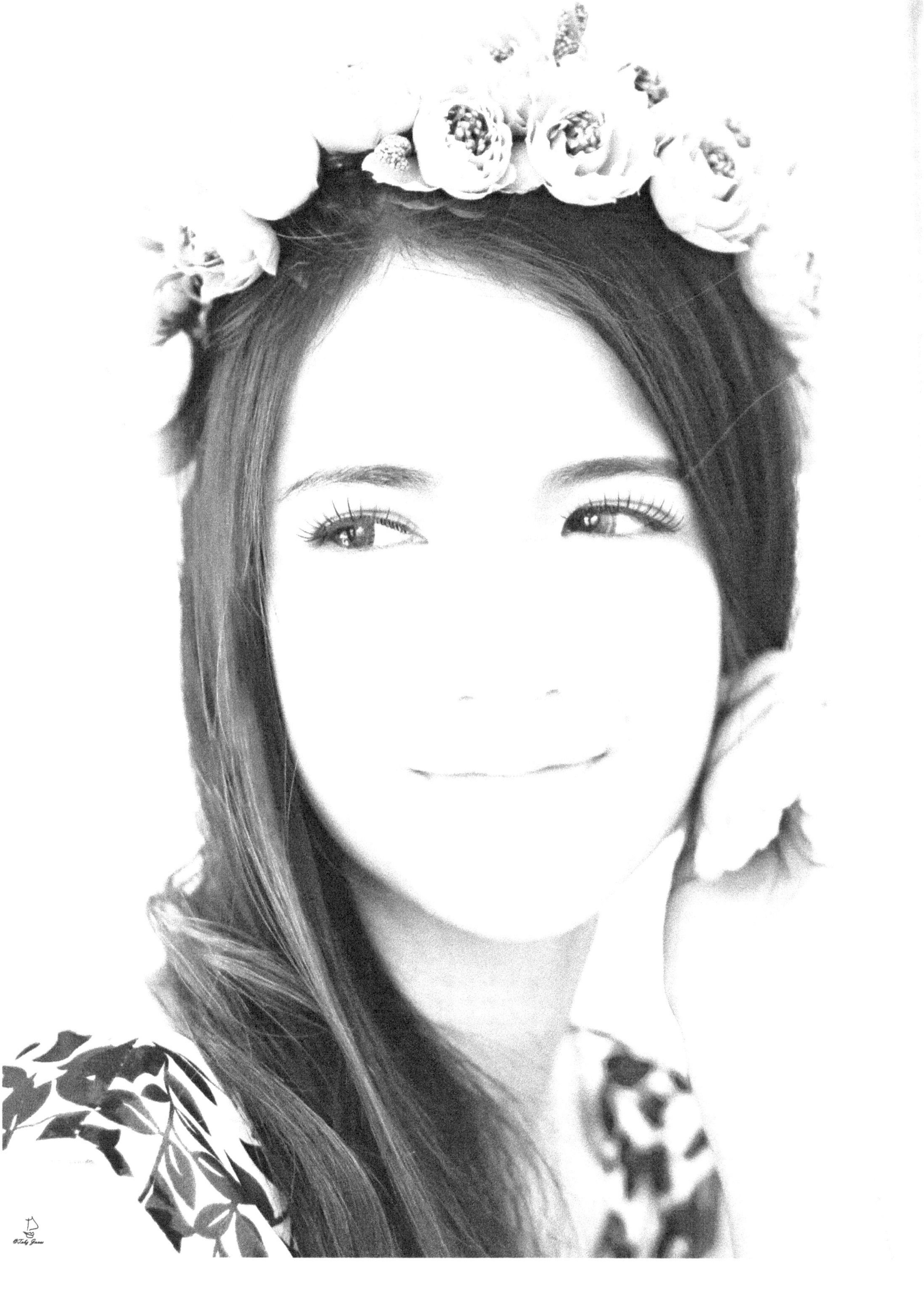

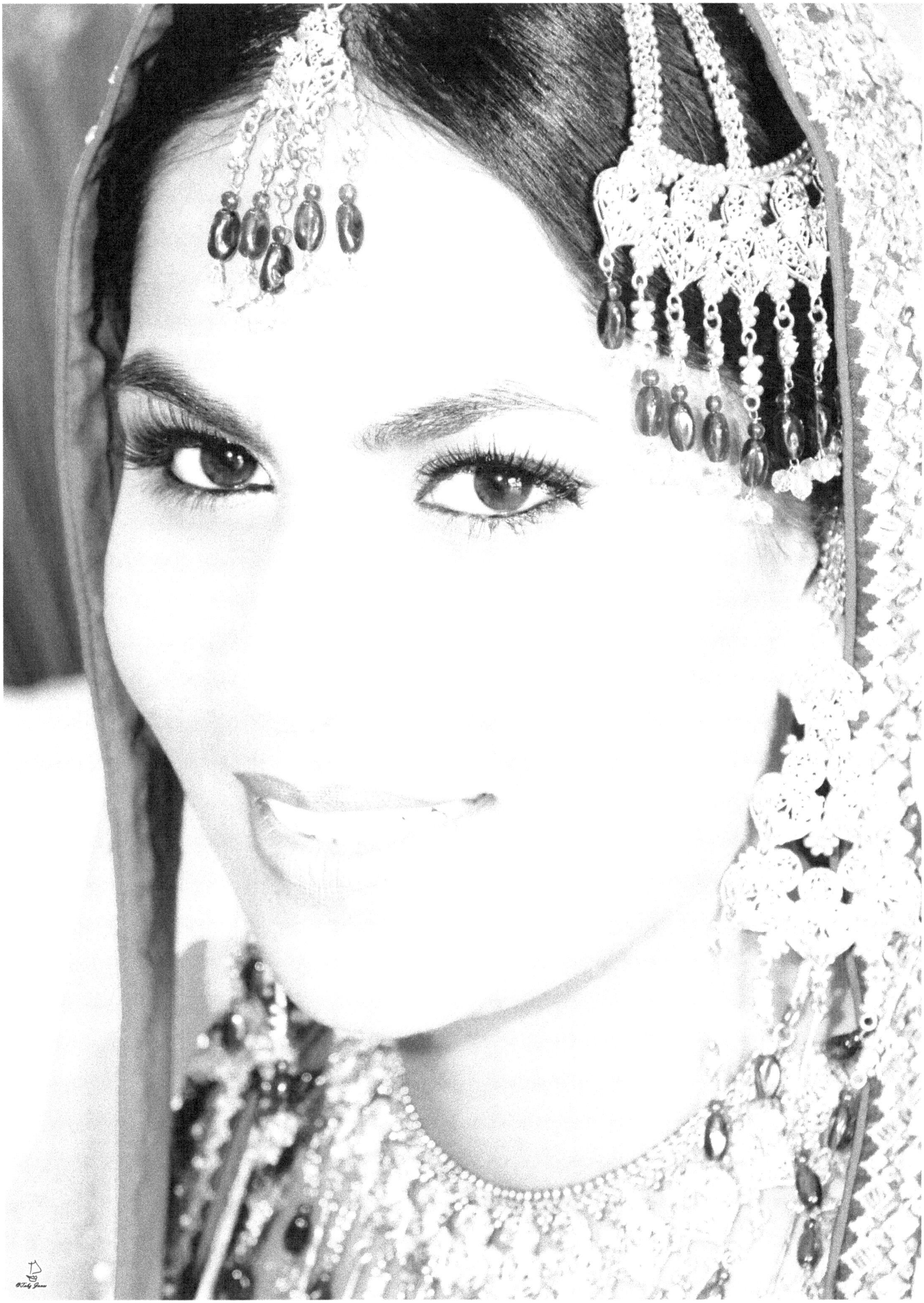

www.ingramcontent.com/pod-product-compliance
Lightning Source LLC
Chambersburg PA
CBHW081906170526
45167CB00007B/3178
* 9 7 8 1 5 4 2 9 5 9 4 5 2 *